I0464725

Notification Of Payment Received

How To Use Internet, Mobile & Social Media Marketing to Turn Clicks Into Clients Customers & Cash!

By

Bro. Bedford, Black America's #1 Internet Marketing & Digital Publishing Coach Consultant & Strategist

Notification Of Payment Received
How to Use Internet, Mobile & Social Media Marketing To Turn Clicks Into Clients, Customers & Cash!

Register This Book and Get Free Updates and Free Videos

To get updates to this book and access to interactive training that will help you implement the strategies in this book to grow your business and an invitation to meet the author, text NOPR to 58885.

Contents

Introduction

Even though I have been asked for years to write a book about the Internet, I was reluctant. I thought long and hard about it and at first, I didn't think it made a lot of sense. Because the Internet is constantly changing and once you have a print book it seemed so final and I didn't want my words to be outdated.

Then, over the years something became crystal clear to me. Yes, the way people use the Internet changes from time to time, however, there are laws and principles that are immutable...they will never change. In fact, they will only become more and more effective as the Internet, Mobile Technology & Social Media grow and traditional marketing and advertising go away.

So in this book you'll find those priceless unchanging principles, that when you implement them they will grow your business and give you the profits you deserve.

And due to the current publishing environment and print-on-demand, I feel very comfortable knowing that those elements that do change from time to time, I can update my work and republish.

For those who already purchased my book, I am making it possible for you to register this book so that I can keep you posted on the latest and greatest changes and resources on a particular subject.

Here is my little piece of advice: use the information and resources in this book. They will help build a tremendous business that you can be proud of and they will help you get more clients and customers which translate into more cash and more freedom.

The biggest difference between average businesses and great businesses boils down to implementation. One implements what they learn while the other procrastinates.

The information that I'm going to provide you in this book works, but it only works for you if you put it to use. Just having this information on your bookshelf or on your desktop will not help you build a great business or get more clients or customers, which will allow you to make more money.

Use it...and send me your success story.

This book has two major objectives:

1) To show you that Your Knowledge, Your Expertise, Your Experience, Your Wisdom, Your Story, Your Passion and Your Message has more value to the world than know and you can take them and turn them into Information Products that you can get paid for.

2) To show you how to effectively use Internet Marketing, Mobile Technology & Social Media to Drive Traffic, Generate Leads, Get More Clients & Customers for practically any business.

I know that those are bold objectives and may even seem unbelievable, especially the part about you turning your knowledge, expertise, experience and passion into information products and getting paid.

I get the unbelievable response often...and it is usually because you aren't aware of this phenomenal industry that exist literally all around us.

There are tens of thousands of people, if not more, who share their knowledge, expertise and advice with the world and get paid for it. Really? These are the people you see on television or hear on radio or on the Internet sharing how to improve your life, relationship, or business.

These are ordinary people who have taken their life's story, research, successes and packaged them in a way that helps people become better parents, relieve stress, build a better business or hundreds of other topics.

You've read their articles, blogs, bought their books, audio programs, DVD home study programs, videos, etc...These programs are not expensive to create and they are easier to create, thanks to the Internet.

These ordinary people have now become well known or famous from sharing their content and advice. They make hundreds of thousands of dollars and some millions of dollars from doing this.

I hear you, "But I'm not famous like them!!" And I ask you to consider, were they famous before they started packaging their information and getting paid or are they famous because they packaged their information.

Sure some were famous before, but more are famous because they made the decision to package their information to help people. All you have to do is make the decision to package who you are and what you know so that you can help people.

You can become influential and have tremendous impact and be highly paid on any topic you choose and that's what I will share with you in the first half of this book.

In the second half of this book I'm going to show you, especially the business owner, how to combine what I share in the first half with modern media and technology to Drive Traffic to existing businesses and websites.

I'm going to show you how to effectively Generate and Capture qualified leads for your business and Convert those leads into paying Clients and Customers. Believe me, this is going to be transformative.

The Internet has reshaped the way we think and conduct business. Communication and content distribution is now free and this allows you to buy, sell or market anything, anywhere, anytime, from any device. The internet and mobile devices have replaced newspapers, radio, television, and even traditional book publishing.

Apple, Google/YouTube, Amazon and Facebook have multibillion dollar distribution networks on the Internet. They literally control the screens, eyes and ears of over 75% of the human population that are engaged on those networks.

If you have a mission or purpose, a product or service, or just a message to get out, there could not be a better time, billions of people are consuming content, clicking links and ads, buying products and services.

This book will introduce you to proven strategies, systems, and training to get on every screen, including television, mobile devices and also in cars. Literally in front of billions of people, so they can find and learn about you, your products and services anytime, anywhere, on any device.

By the time you finish reading this book you'll understand how to reach and connect with over 75% of the human population - who are engaged with social, video and mobile networks right now.

SECTION ONE:

Turn Your Knowledge, Experience, Expertise & Passion

Into Information Products

Chapter One
My Story and Introduction To the World Of
InformationProducts

Let's get straight to the point. I want to stress how important it is that you consider creating your own cash producing Information Products.

If you are thinking of starting an online business, but really don't know what type of business to start or what you can sell, having your own Info Products can be very, very lucrative.

Not only is creating and having your own info products a great way to start a business, but adding information products to an existing business can enhance and possibly save a struggling business.

Information Products have helped businesses I've worked with, giving them different dimension, adding different elements and revenue streams that they never thought possible.

I want to share with you how easy it is to take advantage of this tremendous opportunity and why now is the perfect time.

First, let me tell you what prompted me to start this book out this way.

I was working on the PowerNetworking Conference website. If you don't know, the PowerNetworking Conference is the largest Networking and Business conference for black people on the planet, and it was founded by business icon George Fraser.

George is a mentor and now I can say a friend of mine and I've been presenting at this conference for the past eight years.

I've been working intimately with George and the FraserNet team on the Internet Marketing and other a marketing aspects of the conference.

So as I already mentioned I was working on the conference website and I started noticing the names that I was entering who'll be presenting this year and I started to think about all the names of the people who presented in years past.

Now here I am presenting at this conference sharing this tremendous platform with these giants, these Paragons of Black America, really in the entire world.

And I thought, "Wow!" I'm literally sharing a platform with the likes of Lisa Nichols, Les Brown, Keith Wyche, Michael V. Roberts, Dr. Randal Pinkett, William Patterson, Veronica Conway, Linda Clemons, Pastor Freddie Haynes and many, many more...

Literally dozens and dozens of thought leaders and experts presenting at this conference and I'm sharing this platform with them.

Why is this even important? Why am I mentioning this?

The only reason that I am able to be a part of the faculty for the highly regarded PowerNetworking Conference is because I started creating and developing Information Products and started selling them on the Internet.

That's why I'm stressing to you that if you want to start an Internet business or if you want to take your existing business to new levels you want to begin to turn your own Knowledge, Experience, Expertise, and Passions into products you can sell online.

That's what I started doing years ago.

It started when I went to a conference given be a very famous Real Estate Investor in Orlando, Florida.

Even though this investor made a lot of money buying and selling real estate, this particular conference was about selling Information or what is called Information Marketing.

I was doing well in Real Estate at that time, but it was clear to me that I'd spent thousands of dollars on this

"Guru's" Real Estate courses and trainings and I wanted to know how to do the same.

This investor talked about how he made millions of dollars in real estate but was able to have a global business making millions by teaching others how to invest in real estate.

He sold home study courses, conducted live trainings and held conferences. Needless to say I purchased the home study course on how to do this as well.

I even purchased the rights to sell the actual home study course, which by the way was 16 cassette tapes and a manual. (remember cassette tapes?)

I sold the course and easily made my investment back, but more importantly I studied the course to learn the details of how to make money selling information.

One section of that course really struck a cord with me. It was on how to sell information online, it had not morphed into the term Internet Marketing yet. This was still new way back in early the 2000s.

I followed the training and started building my list by offering a free newsletter. My list grew to around 500 people over a period of a few months.

I then offered my first product which was a small report on a Real Estate technique that I was using. Of course I was super nervous, but I wanted to find out if this Internet stuff really worked.

I wrote an email and sent it out to my list and then I went to sleep. I woke up the next morning and checked my email and noticed that I had several "**Notification Of Payment Received**" in my inbox.

Over the next few days I ended up seeing **212** of those Notification Of Payment Received in my inbox. I sold that report for **$7.00**. Yep a whopping $7.

That was the easiest **$1,400** I'd made in my life up until that point.

After that I was hooked and I began to create dozens of '**Digital Products**' and generated tens of thousands of downloads.

People were asking me questions about entrepreneurship and building a business and I thought if they were asking me they would really love to hear from those more successful than myself.

I got an idea from an existing product and I started interviewing successful 'Black Millionaire Entrepreneurs' to answer those and other questions.

It was called '**Conversations with Black Millionaire**

Entrepreneurs'. This was my breakthrough product and I got national and international attention from this ebook.

This product has taken several different forms over the years and to this day continues to produce traffic, leads, clients, customers, and cash.

I'll share more on this in just a few minutes.

Now here is a great take away for you. I didn't have to come up with the content for the book. All I had to do was ask the questions.

Sure I had to go after the interviews and arrange dates and times, but the answers I received from these successful entrepreneurs was and still is invaluable.

I want you to think about this...I've created this product that will continue to reward me for years and I didn't have to come up with the content.

This is important to understand if you are thinking, "I can't come up with any information to sell" or "People will not pay me for what I know".

You can use the Knowledge, Expertise, or Experience of others. There are a couple of strategies or techniques to do this and I just shared how I interviewed others to create a phenomenal product.

One great result of using this strategy of Interviewing experts to create a product is that others began to view me as an expert, which began to raise my profile with my target audience.

Another great result is I've gotten to know and even become friends with some those that I interviewed and now I've been presenting and sharing the stage with with some of the people I most admired growing up like George Fraser, Dennis Kimbro, Andrew Morrison and others.

One of the other great benefits and truly a blessing is that I've been working with some of these individuals helping them with their Internet Marketing and even partnering on projects.
Back to the main point. This all started first from me going to get the knowledge about this phenomenal and growing industry and implementing what I learned.

I began by starting a newsletter to begin to grow my list. Then I took some information that I possessed and created a little seven dollar report that people could download.

This was over 10 years ago, which seems like a lifetime. Most people don't last long online. If you last 4 or five years you are considered a veteran.

I've been doing it over 10 years and I'm getting better and better. Of course, I've made plenty of mistakes along the way and still make mistakes, but now the mistakes are not as costly.

What Are Information Products

"I hear you Brother Bedford saying how important creating Information Products are to your career and that I should consider it."

"But it feasible?"

"How can I do it?"

"What should be the format?"

Let me deal with these and other questions. Most people are still trying to wrap their minds around what I'm talking about when we talk about Information Products.
What are Information Products?

We are in the 'Information Age' and the time has never been greater for the experienced, successful entrepreneur or the rank beginner to take advantage of the lucrative opportunities that are plentiful in this time.

A whole industry has been born and given life by the ever- increasing pressure and demand on the time of people.

Business people and customers need information provided to them in convenient forms where methods, strategies and research is done for them and in some cases put into easy to follow systems.

There are several different formats for Information Products. There are traditional books, audio programs, video or DVD's which you might buy in a store, catalogs, online and offline magazines, newsletters, e-books, membership web sites, tele-seminars and webinars, online courses, coaching programs, consulting, seminars and conferences, and combinations of any of the above.

I went into my office and I have $100,000 (one hundred thousand dollars) maybe $150,000 (hundred fifty thousand dollars) of info products sitting on my bookshelves.

These are products that I invested in to help make my life better. You've been buying these products all your life or you know others who have purchased audio programs, home study courses, etc…

You just didn't pay attention to the fact that this was an information product that you were consuming that someone else took the time to create and market to you.

We buy these products to make our lives 'Better', 'Easier', or to 'Solve Problems'.

By now I hope you see that you can take your Knowledge, Experience, Expertise, & Passion and create Information Products that you can sell and make more than a living.

The Internet has changed the game completely and made available to you the technology to create and sell your products all over the world with a few clicks.

I shared with you the many different formats you can put your information in. I even shared with you that even if you don't feel you have knowledge that people will buy, you can tap into the Knowledge and Wisdom of others to create products.

I hope you see that the time and the technology has never been better and more accessible.

I think I answered those earlier questions...

"Is it feasible?" **Yes**

"Can I do it?" **Yes**

"The different formats?" **Traditional books, audio programs, video or DVD's which you might buy in a store, catalogs, online and offline magazines, news-**

letters, e-books, membership web sites, tele-seminars and webinars, online courses, coaching programs, consulting, seminars and conferences, and combinations of any of the above.

In the next chapter I'm going to show you the money. Once you see how much money can be made and the relatively small number of sales needed to achieve certain goals, you'll see why creating your own Information Products is a no-brainer.

Chapter Two
Show Me The Money

"Ok Bro. Bedford. This Creating and Selling Information Products to start or grow my business sounds very interesting, but can you really make money?"

Absolutely! I wanna show you the math to a **$50,000** (fifty thousand dollar) income selling your own information products.

You may ask, "where did I get $50,000 from?" I don't know.

I thought it was a good number that if you are just starting a business, it's a good goal to shoot for.

If you already have a business, an extra $50,000 revenue stream can mean a world of difference for your business.

Of course if you want to make more money, you'll soon know the formula to scale up to do that, it won't be that difficult and if you want to make less all you have to do is just scale back your efforts.

Ok, so let me show you the money.

I showed you quite a few different formats for your information products in the last chapter. I won't cover them all now, but you'll get the picture.

Audio Programs:
One of the formats I showed you was Audio Programs. A nice audio program can consist of **4, 5,** or **6 CDs.**

Let's say that you create a 6 Cd audio program and you're selling that audio program for **$197.** All you would need is 254 audio programs sold to make $50,038 in a year.

If you break that down further, divide those 254 products down by 12 months. That means that you only have to sell 21 audio programs per month to achieve a little over a $50,000 income. That's not a lot to sell, especially with the entire planet as potential customers.

Audio Programs
$197 x 254= $50,038
254 divided by 12 = 21/per month

DVD Programs:
Video has a higher perceived value than audio. You can sell a **4** or **6 DVD Program** for **$297.**

You would need to sell 169 DVD Programs at $297 to make $50,193 a year. That's only 14 programs a month. Do you think that if you put your mind to it you could sell 14 programs a month.

DVD Programs
$297 x 169= $50,193
169 divided by 12 = 14/per month

Home Study Course:
I have some Home Study Courses that range from
$2,000 to $5,000.

Just in case you are arguing saying, "I can't create a
course that will cost that much…" Let's keep it simple
and say you charge **$497 for your course** that may
include manuals, with DVDs or CDs or something like
that.

To make a $50,000 income for the year all you would
need to sell is 101(one hundred and one) $497 Home
Study Course to $50,197. If you divide that by 12 that
means that you would have to sell 8 courses a month to
make the goal. 8 courses a month.

Home Study Course Programs
$497 x 101= $50,197
101 divided by 12 = 8/per month

Ebooks, Manuals & Guides
Let's move on to some 'Digital Products'. Let's say you
sold in ebook or manual for **$27,** I'm talking about you
selling direct downloads. Selling ebooks on Amazon is
different and I'll talk about that later.

When I first started there wasn't an Amazon and we sold ebooks, which were PDF's that we called 'Special Reports' or 'Training Manuals' for $27, $47 or more. The strategy still works today if done properly.

Let's get back to the math. If you sold a ebook, special report, manual, or guide for $27 in order to achieve a $50,000 you need to sell 1,852 of those e-books, manuals, reports or guides.

Now if you divide that by 12 that means that you have to sell 154 a month. You may be thinking 154 down-loads a month is a lot. When you're online and you're dealing with the entire world, 154 people download-ing in ebook, report, manual or some type of guide from you is not a lot of people.

In fact, you may already have thousands following you on Twitter or Facebook. So look at the power of these numbers, just 1,852 people over the course of year downloading your ebooks, manuals, reports, or guides at $27 will give you a $50,000 income.

Ebooks, Manuals, Reports or Guides
$27 x 1852 = $50,004
1852 divided by 12 = 154/per month

Tele-Seminars
Let's talk about tele-seminars. What is a Tele-Seminar? Tele-seminars are where you are talking to people on

the telephone, teaching them, training them or giving some type a special information that they would pay money for.

The technology used for this is called a Conference Call or Bridge Line.

You can have just one seminar or it could be a series with 2, 3 or 4 seminars together or maybe 2 or 3 a day.
Let's do the math. You can charge $47 for your tele-seminar or series of seminars. You would need 1,064 people for the entire year to make $50,008. Now divide that 1,064 people by 12, that means that you would need 89 callers per month paying $47 for you to have a $50,000 income.

Tele-Seminars
$47 x 1064 = $50,008
1064 divided by 12 = 89/per month

Webinars
Webinars are extremely popular now and their popularity has made them easier to conduct and more valuable in the eyes of consumers today than ever before.

What are webinars? Similar to tele-seminars except webinars are done through your computer where people can see you or a presentation through your webcam or other camera.

The technology to host webinars has become very affordable today. You have Go To Meeting or Go To Webinar. There are also other software options that allow you use them in connection with LiveStream, UStream, YouTube Live and Google Hangouts.

Using YouTube Live and Google Hangouts is FREE! I'll talk more in depth about YouTube Live and Google Hangouts in the second half of this book.

A webinar can be just you on camera or delivering a presentation or you can have special guests teaching people, training them or giving some type a special information that people would be interested in and that they would pay money for.

Let's say you charge $97 for your webinar. All you would need is 516 people for an entire year to generate $50,052. 516 people divided by 12 means that you would only have to have 43 people per month register for your webinars to generate a $50,000 income.

Webinars
$97 x 516 = $50,052
516 divided by 12 = 43/per month

Online Courses/Training
Let's look at online courses or training. Everyone is providing online courses. Oprah Winfrey is providing

online courses and training, so are some of your larger magazine providers and business trainers providing online courses or training.

This is not as strange as it used to be when I first started years ago. To talk about delivering training online or an online course seemed so foreign then, but now it's common.

In fact, the whole educational model for colleges and universities, private and public schools are going online for homework and supplemental education. So people are not freaked out when you start talking about delivering information, training or knowledge in online environment.

More and more people are receptive to it because now a person can sit in their own home and consume the materials or the content that they want and they don't mind paying for it and they can go at their own pace.

There are just so many advantages to doing this but let's get back to the numbers. If you deliver an online course or training for $147, you only need 341 people for an entire year to enroll in your online course for you to generate a $50,000 income.

Divide 341 people by 12 and that's 28 registrants per month in order for you to generate $50,000.

Online Courses/Training
$147 x 341 = $50,127
341 divided by 12 = 28 registrants/per month

Membership Sites/Subscription Program
I am a big fan of membership programs and subscription programs.

I want you to imagine this... You have a subscription program that pays you $47 a month. The subscription program could be something like a CD of the month or DVD of the month.

So that you won't think this is new or out of the ordinary, you've heard of book of the month clubs, magazine subscriptions or newsletter subscriptions.

Your cable bill and your phone bill are built on the subscription model or the membership model or the recurring revenue model.

Let's get back to the numbers. There are a couple ways to look at this. If you want to make a $50,000 income and you want to use this model...you can deliver content through a membership site or through the mail or online monthly access for a one time fee of $47.

All you need is 1064 people for the entire year to enroll in your program to make $50,008. 1064 divided by 12 is 89 new members per month. But now watch the power of the membership or subscription model.

You can actually make a $50,000 income with only 89 people paying you $47 a month. That's $4,183 a month in revenue coming from those 89 people who are in ongoing program. That's $50,196 in income.

That's why I love membership programs or subscription models because it's it provides you monthly revenue or monthly cash flow. And if you do it right you won't have to continually create content.

Membership/Subscription Programs
$47 x 1064 = $50,008
1064 divided by 12 = 89 members/subscribers
or 89 x $47 = $4,183 per month

I know by now you see the possibilities of turning your Knowledge, Expertise, Experience, or Passion into Information Products.
Let me show you the money to one more model.

Coaching Sessions
Nowadays people are doing one-on-one coaching sessions online via tools like Skype and Google Hangouts. You can also do one-on-one coaching over the phone.

Let's just say you have a product or service or business where you do extremely well, but you never thought to add coaching to your business.

You would be surprised to know that some of your existing customers are already desirous of your coaching but you never offered it to them.

Let's just say you charged $997 for coaching sessions with you, all you would need is 51 people to coach for an entire year for you to make a $50,000 income.

That's only 4 clients a month, that's 1 person a week. If you are you able to generate one client a week that would be $50,847 in income.

Okay, I want to close this section out, but I just wanted to "Show You The Money". And there are variations of all these programs that you can implement.

I just wanted to give you an idea of 'What You Can Do' 'How You Make Money' by Selling Information Products.

In the next chapter I'm going to show you the 'Best Way' to sell your Information Products online.

Chapter Three
The Best Way To Sell Online

I hope by now you are able to wrap your mind around this idea of Turning Your Knowledge, Experience, Expertise & Passion into Information Products.

You and I have been consuming these products all our lives and if we haven't consumed these Information Products ourselves, we know someone who has.

People purchase these products to learn some specialized training to help them in their business or to get some help with their golf game and they don't mind paying good money for that.

So I've been attempting to show you how this business is all around us, but we've never really taken the time to focus on it...

But more importantly we've never really taken the time to see ourselves on the other end providing that information, providing that training, providing that education.

We sometimes can't see ourselves providing messages that help people better their lives and better their businesses.

Whether it's relationships or cooking...you name it, there is not an industry where information products are not present and people are making a lot of money providing that information to individuals in those niches and in those categories.

Now I'm going to show you the best way to sell your information products or better stated, I'm going to show you the process to sell your information products.

In truth, this is the best way to sell anything online.

The Internet has changed the way the world conducts business. My job isn't to tell you that you need a web presence online, you already know that you need a web presence.

Most people have started to have a web presence whether it's a website or their on FaceBook, Twitter or some other platform.

The problem is just having a website or being on Face-Book does not translate into making sells. That's why I said that I'm going to show you the process, which is more than a website.

In truth, having a website by itself is the worst way to sell information products and products in general. I want you to start thinking in terms of 'Pages' and not website.

When you are selling your information products there are functions that must take place in order for your potential customer or client to part with their hard earned money.

And traditional websites sometimes can't provide these functions for you effectively.

The first function is to add value. When visitors visit your site they want to see something that adds value to their lives. This can be blog post articles, audios and videos.

They don't want to see you bragging about yourself and talking about how much you're charging for products and how big your car and house is.

They want content and training and it is your job to give it to them for free, in order to build rapport and provide value to them.

The second function is to capture leads. If you are providing value then it is only a matter of time before more and more people visit your site and you should be capturing their name and email.

You do this by offering free training, resources or a gift in exchange for their name and email. The is not new, you've seen this before when you see an offer to sign up for a Newsletter to receive more goodies...

Capturing leads to build your list is critical for your long-term success. In the online world having a list and a great relationship with that list is directly related to your income and influence.

Once you have a person's contact information, you can continue to send them more value, deepen your relationship, and offer them your products, programs, and services.

The third function is to make money. I know this seems obvious, but I have dealt with hundreds of entrepreneurs and business owners whose sites fail to effectively feature and sell their products, programs, and services.

In fact, most entrepreneurs and business owners say that their websites fail miserably doing these three things. The truth is most traditional websites are not designed to complete all the functions.

This is why I said to you to start thinking in terms of 'Pages' instead of 'websites'. So now let me share with you what I mean by pages and further explain the process.

What are Pages?

When you go to a traditional website it is made up of different pages. There's the Home Page, the About

Page, Contact Page, etc...

As you can see those pages are designed to give basic information, but not much else. Traditional websites allow for people to just browse around, there isn't an isolation of the pages and they don't force the visitors to do anything, but leave. And that is a problem.

In today's online environment people want value when the visit a site, they want engagement and in most cases they are searching for specific information.

That's why you should have what's called an 'Opt-In' Page or a 'Landing Page'.

An opt-in page or a landing page typically has one specific message with an offer to exchange something of value (preferably what your visitor wants) for their name and email.

There aren't options for them to click around on your site. It's really simple, "If you want the 'Free Gift' I have for you just enter your name and email and sometimes a mobile number (I'll get into this later) I will send you the gift.

Now before you say, "email is dead, nobody uses email anymore". Let me assure you that email is not dead, in fact email is more important than your Facebook, twitter, Linkedin, and any other social media you have combined.

When I ask people what do you use to login to your Facebook and other Social Media...they say "duh... my email".

People began to think that email was not important because Facebook began to get popular and everything begin to move into mobile. Now the Facebook craze has normalized and people receive email directly to their mobile phones now.

So email or should I say having the email of your prospects is critical to your online success. You must build your own list. I'll talk more about this later in this book.

Let's get back to the process. After a visitor gives you their name and email they are directed to a Thank You Page or a Download Page to receive the 'Valuable Gift' you promised them.

Now you can connect and engage with them in an ongoing process. The next step is to send them more valuable content to further build and establish a relationship.

You send them an email sending them to the next page which I call a 'Value Piece'. Why value piece? On this page will be more value either helping the individual or solving a problem.

This helps the recipient to begin to 'like' you and 'trust' you because you are helping them by providing value first. On this page can be either a video, audio or a .pdf download.

Can you just put the value in the email...yes, but you want to engage your potential customer or client. The more interaction and engagement they take, the more they trust that you are the solution to their problem.

What next? Send them another 'Value Piece'. I suggest sending around 3 'Value Pieces' before you ask for a sale. In fact, each piece should be building more anticipation for your sale.

After your third 'Value Piece' now you can send them to your 'Sales Page' which is specifically designed to sale your product or service.

Can't you see how this process with pages covers those 3 functions of:

1) Capturing Leads 2) Adding Value 3) Making Money

This is much better than just trying to get people to buy from a website that is not designed to sale.

Most people will tell you that their websites are terrible at doing these 3 things. That is why I wanted to share with you or whoever you have doing your website this process.

You may be saying to yourself, "I get it now, I can turn my Knowledge, Experience, Expertise, & Passion into Information Products and sell them online, but how do I get people to my opt-in page or other pages".

Essentially you're saying, "How do I get Traffic and Leads to me and my products and services". I'm going to go into that and the 'Ultimate' way to sell anything online in the second section of this book.

SECTION TWO

**How To Use Internet Marketing,
Mobile Technology & Social Media
to Drive Traffic, Capture Leads,
Get More Clients & Customers
For Any Business**

Chapter Four
A New Era

If you have a business or you've been marketing a product or service you already know that television, radio and traditional media are dying.

Truth be told old fashioned Internet, social media, blogging and content marketing isn't working as well as it used to either.

The good news is there are some exciting new ways to market your business, products, and services that give you nearly unlimited reach and a unique way to interact with your ideal customers and clients...

In the second half of this book I'm going to reveal to you the new technology and new media showing you **EXACTLY** where the market is headed and how you can finally use it to sell more products, build your brand and engage your following.

The old days of SEO (search engine optimization) and broadcasting online are over.

You used to just be able to create any type of content and blast it all over the internet, get links back to your site and get some results.

That doesn't work anymore, you can't depend on SEO.

These days it's all about getting targeted messages to the right Channels.

That's a big part of what we're going to cover in this book.

Now let me give you a few stats that you might find relevant.

As of this writing...

Every minute **Pinterest** users post **3500 images.**
YouTube users upload over **72 Hours of video every minute.**
Vine users share over **8,333 videos per minute.**
Facebook users share over **2 and half million pieces of content** every minute.
Twitter users tweet **277,000 times** per min.
Apple users download **48,000 apps** per min.
Pandora users listen to **62,000 hours** of music per min.
Instagram users post **216,000 new photos** per min.
Email users send **204 Million messages** per min.
Skype users connect for over **23,000 hours** per min.

I could go on and on, but I think you get the picture.

Why is this relevant to you?

Well, as you can see there are all of these different types of channels and Google search doesn't matter as much as it use to.

More data is moving around the entire world thru mobile apps than through the Internet or browsers. Let me say that another way.

Over half of all online activity is happening through mobile apps or as I like to say, "Channels" instead of regular desktop searches.

What does that mean to you?

As a business owner, entrepreneur, service provider, professional, if you want to get and keep the attention of your customers or clients, you've got to be thinking about what channel you are broadcasting your message to and how it is being consumed.

So if you're not creating mobile compatible content and delivering to channels and locations online that are accessible through apps, you're missing out on more than half of all online users.

This is why you hear some say that "online marketing" isn't working like it used to and regular search or SEO is becoming less relevant.

It's all about creating compelling and engaging content. That's what a huge part of this book is about.

How to Get and Keep Attention...how to engage and build relationships and get people to want to buy from you.

Once you're able to do this you will stand out, you will earn the market and nothing can be done to take that away from you

Chapter Five
The Biggest Business Marketing Challenge!

Your biggest business marketing challenge is Getting and Keeping Attention!

Now let's deal with the reason why you can't cut through all of the clutter to get the attention your business deserves.

I'm going to address this first from a consumer's point of view and then from the entrepreneur's or business owner's view.

It stems from a simple premise...

The amount of **Information is way Out of Control!**

We being members of a **'Digital World'** are getting crushed under a wave of too much information. And that information overload is having an unfavorable and serious impact on the world making the "attention" of your prospects' more valuable than ever for your business.

There are several factors as to why we suddenly find ourselves paralyzed by too much information.

Factor #1). Too Much Information to Process.

We are just being bombarded with more information than we can possibly process. The amount of information that gets thrown at us is constantly expanding.

As of the middle of 2015 the internet has well over three **BILLION** Internet users and that creates a target rich environment for every content/information provider and marketer in the world.

Not only do we have this flooded environment of information and providers, the channels through which that information overload flows has expanded also!

Factor #2) We Are Bombarded with Unsolicited Information

And the problem isn't just information. We are constantly distracted by information we don't even want! Technology has evolved to try to rein this in with things like caller ID to more advanced technology like email service providers' filtering algorithms and search engines tailoring their results to be as relevant to you as possible. Still marketers continue to find ways to keep dumping more information on you.

Factor #3). The Speed of Information is Crushing Us!

All the information is coming faster and faster and there is nothing that points to slowing it down either.

Years ago downloading an image could take up to 5 to 10 minutes. The bigger bandwidth and faster processors have made those wait times a thing of the past, but with this speed, we've shrunk our tolerance to wait for anything.

This increase in speed has made us more "instant gratification" oriented. We get frustrated faster. We give up more easily and we're more inclined to just walk away.

I know we can never go back to slow. But faster isn't helping us focus either.

Factor #4). We Place Less Value on the Information We Have

With all of this information that is out here, the supply is simply more than the demand. The law of Supply and Demand makes us to place less value on information.

The only exception is information we get that is Specifically Important to us. This leads us to another attention-based obstacle. And that is finding **EXACTLY** what you're looking for before you get frustrated (or even worse — distracted) and just give up.

Factor #5). Contradictory Information!

For every person saying one thing, there is another person trying to get your attention saying the complete opposite. And of course all these "Guru's" supposedly know more than you do. This is why there is so much Confusion and most people feel Frustrated.

Factor #6). Our Information Needs Keep Changing

Depending on what new technology you try to incorporate into your life or business will determine what type and how much information will be required to keep up with the latest developments.

However, that requirement for information has actually fragmented. Older people want "simpler" and are not wanting to battle to keep up with the latest advances in technology.

While later generations are more likely to welcome and take on more innovating technology (and consequently more information). We have children who have no knowledge whatsoever of a world without personal digital media. And their needs for more information have become more specialized.

Now as Entrepreneurs, Business Owners, Professionals, and Service Providers we have to become Masters of This Era.

Since the beginning of time, entrepreneurs have always found ways to enhance your economic value to the world. You mastered the skills you needed to make yourself more prominent, more important and more wealthy.

Even back in the stone age...When your economic value was based solely on whether or not you were able to hunt and kill stuff.

You Mastered it!

Next was the Agricultural age. A time when your economic success was based on land ownership and your farming skills.

You Mastered It!

Next was the Industrial Age. This was the era of assembly lines and mass production. In this era your economic value was determined by how much and how efficiently you could produce and deliver anything.

You Mastered it!

Next was the Information Age. In this time computers and satellites have given the world unlimited access to information. And your economic value came from how much you knew. This is where the phrase "Knowledge is Power" began to resonate.

You Mastered It!

Now as the information age matures, we have found ourselves in what I call 'The Age Of Connectivity'. This is where technology has begun to link us all together.

During this era, your economic advantage will come from your ability to reach out and inject yourself into the lives of your prospects.

So it should be clear that in every era your success depends on the particular skills you master. But the bottom line is your ultimate success depends how well you adapt to the requirements of the age you live in now.

In every era throughout history you have an opportunity to enhance your economic value in whatever it is you're doing. You just have to keep up with the times.

And in this era where it is getting harder and harder to get and keep attention, you need to leverage the tools and strategies that work best.

If you don't, you're headed for trouble.

The environment has changed. The rules of the game have changed, and many of us are struggling. We are still trying to enhance our economic value by doing what we were doing five years ago.

In this new era, all the traditional means of gaining an economic advantage have fallen by the wayside.

None of the things we did then are working and will not work.

So what's the bottom line?

How do you stand out? How do you get noticed and attract a steady stream of prospective buyers in an era when the next distraction could derail all your efforts?

You Must Master...

Commanding Your Market's
Attention and Keeping that attention.

You may be asking, *"Bro. Bedford how do I command my market's attention and then keep that attention?"*

There will be some who will tell you that you can make a bunch of noise a broadcast silly, "cutting edge" marketing materials.

Better yet why not make over-the-top promises that no one will believe.

Or you can give away free irrelevant content. And give and give and give until there's nothing left.

You can spend a ton of money on "brand recognition" that may or may not connect you to your prospective market.

The bottom line is whether you give away free content or spend a ton on brand recognition the goal is to 'Get Traffic'.

In truth, the most straight forward, efficient way to get traffic is to ...

Buy it.

What?

That's right. You can absolutely buy all the attention you want.

But we know that's not the end of the discussion. Simply "getting" attention isn't enough.

That's why I said, "You have to master commanding Attention!"

And commanding attention is not the same thing. Not even close.

Commanding your market's attention means getting and **KEEPING** that attention.

And keeping attention, once you've got it, is a whole new ball game.

That's why making a bunch of noise, shouting, over-the-top promises and irrelevant freebies won't make someone stick around for long. (At least not the people you want to stick around.)

Commanding the attention of your market means they are engaged with you. Interacting with you. Not just liking your Facebook page or leaving comments on your blog.

You do this by providing maximum value. Creating and distributing compelling and engaging content. I'm going to go deeper on this in a later chapter of this book.

The proof that you have 'commanded your prospects attention' properly is they will spend money with your business.

Getting and Keeping your prospect's attention is done through the mechanism of your business.

So you have to make sure you have an attention-worthy business with the right strategy and pieces in place to monetize the attention you get.

We don't have enough space to go into the 'Design of Your Business'. The purpose of the this book is to show you how to Get and Keep Attention and make more sales.

But a well designed Business will maximize the value of all of this new attention you will be receiving.

Now let's dive into how your going to Get and Keep this attention...

Chapter Six
How To Leverage Billion Dollar Platforms and Reach Billions Of People For Free!

I have some very important information that I want to share with entrepreneurs, business owners, professionals, speakers, coaches and consultants on what I've been doing and what I've been working on behind the scenes with some very well established businesses; helping them to grow their business.

We have entered into a very interesting time. Most people consider this the greatest time in human history.

With all of the developments, the cataclysmic events, all of the tragedies, the wars, everything that we're witnessing…there's a phenomenon present that brings all of this to our eyes and ears in a matter of minutes, sometimes seconds.

I'm talking about the Internet and Mobile Technology.

This technology is impacting the lives of billions of people. Governments have been overthrown by the power of the Internet. Businesses have been transformed by the power of the Internet.

I've been on doing Internet Marketing for over 10 years now. Every year it has increased in its effectiveness. There have been all types of new gadgets that come and go.

There are new technologies, new platforms, that weren't in existence 10 years ago that are common now. It has been a phenomenal experience for all of us who have been able to grab hold to the technology and use the Internet properly to really grow our businesses.

More entrepreneurs are able to start their businesses from the comforts of their own home simply by having a laptop and Internet connection and maybe a webcam. Some don't even need an external webcam because your computer comes with one.

You don't need elaborate offices nowadays. There's nothing wrong with having an office, but you can literally work from a coffee shop with an Internet connection.

More entrepreneurs are being birthed at a rapid rate from their home, their garages, and their basements. I'm not just talking about the United States of America.

We're talking about all over the globe. It has never been easier for you to create content and have it distributed all over the world in with just the click of a button.

I have coached and consulted with, literally hundreds of entrepreneurs over the last few years and I've been able to help them become more efficient in using this "new technology", the Internet, to Turn Clicks into Clients, Customers and Cash!

With this simple and affordable technology, you can have your message, your products, and services seen, heard, shared, and even put in the pockets of the people you want to reach.

You may not believe it, but your message can be viewed or listened to on billions of mobile devices, computers, televisions and even in the cars of millions of people or businesses in the world with the click of a button — and all of this can be done **FOR FREE.**

If you know how to create compelling and engaging content, the biggest brands in the world...Google, Apple, Amazon, Facebook, YouTube, Twitter, LinkedIn will market and promote you and share your message with the world for free - and the tip me over is that some will promote and pay you for that privilege.

I'm going to show you how to partner with Google and iTunes. I'm going to show you how any business or professional can use the internet to Turn their Clicks into Clients, Customers and Cash.

I've already talked about the power of the internet. I'm going to show you how to use this technology to create compelling content and to deliver the content.

I'm going to show you how to generate and capture leads and turn those leads into prospects and those prospects into clients, customers and ultimately the result of having clients and customers is cash.

I'm going to show you how to use these strategies, these tools and these resources to partner with these billion dollar brands. No longer do you have to be concerned with you being able to get your message out to the public.

Once we do this you're going to be able to build engaging lists of prospects and customers and really be able to have your business growing at an astounding rate with some of the things that I'm going to share with you.

The beautiful part is that you can do these important and fantastic things with tools you already have... your smartphone, a computer, maybe a webcam and a simple microphone.

You can distribute your content everywhere on every mobile device, on every laptop, on smart televisions, in cars, all those things with these simple tools.

You may be thinking, "Bro. Bedford, that is some big and bold stuff you're talking there". It is but I'm going to prove it to you. You have to understand that in the past the media was out of our control.

Today, the media is in our control. When we're talking about YouTube, Google, Facebook, Twitter, all of these social media outlets they're right here at our fingertips.

Here has been the problem for business owners and professionals. To create engaging and compelling content and distribute it to all of these channels can take too much time to implement and can take too much money to hire someone.

Some of us have blown a lot of money trying to build an Internet presence by hiring web and graphic designers to create logos and build outdated websites that didn't work out.

The other problem is the tech knowledge has been absent for most people. If you have a business and you're working on your business, you don't really have the time to try to learn all of the technologies that you need to really grow your business.

Learning the technology or even having the right type of people who can help you to implement the technology or even have the tech knowledge to really grow your business, has been a problem.

I'm going to solve that problem.

That's my job. That's why you're reading this book. My job is to show you the simple strategies and tools to create content - engaging and compelling content. I want to keep stressing I'm not just talking about any type of content. We're talking about engaging and compelling content.

I'm going to show you how to promote your business, your products, your service and your brand. By leveraging these billion dollar businesses, these billion dollar brands. This is going to really help to explode your business. And you're going to be able to do all of this without having to be a tech genius, okay?

I know that this sounds good, but I must confess to you that if you don't possess 3 qualities, then what I'm sharing with you will not work.

Here are the three qualities you must possess in order to for these strategies to work for you and in order for these Billion Dollar Brands to partner and promote you.

You must have a burning desire serve and improve someone else's life. You have to want to help people.

You have to have a desire to share your views and answer questions or be willing to get the views, opinions, and answers from other experts.

Your potential clients and customers have problems that they need answers and solutions to, and you have to be able to deliver those answers or at least engage with experts who can.

You have the desire to give away and share these views and answers. This is where a lot of businesses that I've consulted over the past few years have really had big problems.

They want to hold the information to try to get their clients or customers or potential customers to pay money. You don't want to educate your client or your customer and then you're wondering why they're not buying.

You can't fear giving away your best stuff, thinking that people won't buy. The opposite is true. By giving away "your best stuff", you have an opportunity to to build relationships and influence. I'm sure you've heard, "you don't get a second chance to make a first impression."

For some strange reasons, we've fallen into this thought of "just buy my stuff, just buy my stuff, just look at it and buy my stuff" and that doesn't work.

That's what we do as entrepreneurs. We solve problems. If we possess these qualities where we like to help people, we're always solving problems or providing solutions to whatever it is that they are encountering and sharing it puts us head and shoulders above "competition".

"Ok, Bro. Bedford, this sounds awesome, but how do I answer those questions, share my views and partner with these Billion Dollar Brands?"

Ok, I hear you just walk with me.

Here's something that you may not realize, you have a studio in your pocket. If you are a professional, chances are you have a smartphone. You are literally walking around with the production studio in your pocket that shoots high definition video and can also record high quality audio.

The type of video that this smart phone is shooting nowadays is equivalent to the cameras of seven to eight years ago where we used to have to pay $10,000 to get a camera to shoot high definition video. Now we're walking around and we're able to do this anytime we want.

I'm going to show you how to use that to build an active audience. I'm going to show you how to use that to get seen and heard and distributed on all of these billion dollar brands that we've talked about. The key is creating, engaging and compelling content.

Now before I share with you how to create this engaging and compelling content, first, let me give you some interesting statistics to lay the framework for why it is so important for you to utilize these new strategies and technologies in your business and your profession.

As of this writing, there are close to **(15) Fifteen Billion Mobile Accounts in use.**

There are **(2) Two to (3) Three Billion Smart Phones** that are in usage.

There are **300 Million Smart TVs** and that's expected to be **400 Million by the end of the year, that's growing extremely fast.**

There are **(2) Two Billion Tablets** in use and that's expected to be **(3) Three Billion Tablets** very soon.

Even with tablets out selling desktop computers by a margin of three to one, there's still (3) Three Billion Connected Desktop Computers on the planet.

Here's something else, **96 Million people drive to work every day** an average of 40 to 45 minutes in their cars. (20%) Twenty Percent of those people are listening to streaming services.

You may already be listening to streaming services on your commute to your office or to your workplace or just working out and this is including Podcast.

Podcasts Are Exploding at a phenomenal rate. That's one of the reasons why you want to use this new technology and begin to add things like podcast to your platform by creating compelling content. I'll talk more about this later.

With all of these things that I've just told you, with all of the mobile connections, all the accounts and what's happening with people driving and listening to streaming devices, the smart televisions, and tablets...you can see the world's population is connected.

We've seen this connection have major political impact, but most business owners have not discovered how to get maximum impact yet.

What if Google promoted you? What would that do for your business? What if Apple promoted you? What if Amazon promoted you? What would that do to your business? And of course Facebook and Twitter.

Some are already saying, "*I'm already on Facebook.*" I know, I know just stay with me.

Let me give you a few more statistics to drive home the point of why you want these brands to promote you and why they want to promote you.

Why do you want to be on the devices that Apple presents to everyone or to the world?

They have **500 Million Credit Cards on file.** Over **1.3 billion users** who spend an average of **$330 a year.**

These are user accounts on file looking for engaging and compelling content.

They have nearly **1.5 Billion Podcast Subscribers.** Can you imagine the possibility of your message reaching Apples massive customer base.

Let's talk about **Google, YouTube** and **Android.**

There are over **425 Million Gmail Users**
300 Million Google+ Users.
There are **(1) One Billion YouTube Accounts**
 (4) Four Million Video views a day.

What about **Amazon?**

They have over **220 Million Credit Cards on file.**
They have over **20 Million Prime Users** who spend an average of **$1,224 a year.**

When I mentioned this at a recent conference where I was speaking, over half the room agreed because they were prime members already and they knew that they were spending that type of money every year.

Let's list a few more...

Facebook has 1.23 billion active of monthly users.
Yahoo - 281 million accounts.
Twitter - 243 of active monthly users.
LinkedIn - 277 million.

As I mentioned earlier **over 75% of the human popu-**
lation is connected and engaged in social media.

And these big brands want you to create engaging
and compelling content and in return they will allow
you to engage and sale to their customers.

You may be thinking, "*Why would they do that?*"

Because **Apple sells more movies, music, television**
shows, phones and iPhones when they have people
engaged on their platforms.

Facebook and **Google sell more ads when people**
use their platforms. Amazon sells more books and
of course physical products.

How do you and I partner with them? We simply give
them what they want...and that is **interesting, engag-**
ing and compelling content.

Chapter Seven
How To Create Engaging & Compelling Content and the Psychology Behind It!

In this chapter I'm going to talk to you not only about creating engaging and compelling content, but also content that is entertaining and educational.

When you create engaging, compelling, entertaining, and educational content, you'll be able to market your personal brand, your company, or your products and services to millions of people all over the world - for free!

When you do this correctly you will be accessible on every mobile device your target customer owns and at the same time leveraging the biggest brands in the world.

Can you imagine your visibility and the ability to grow your list when you learn how to partner with companies like Google, Amazon, Facebook, Twitter, Apple, You-Tube, LinkedIn, and more...

You have the opportunity to get published on major platforms including major blogs, newspapers, and magazines. You have the opportunity to have your own television and radio shows.

I'll talk about this and more in the next chapter. You're going to be surprised at the power this will give you when you start looking at the marketing of your business through this new lens.

Ok, now before we get into the formula for creating engaging, compelling, entertaining, and educational content...I want to ask you, "What business are you in?"

When I ask this question, I get all types of answers. People would say, "I'm a hair stylist, or I'm a financial planner, or a dance teacher, or a health practitioner."

Some of the more seasoned business owners would say, "I'm in the Marketing Business" and that would have been my answer up until a few years ago. I used to say that I am in the marketing business.

But that changed because I realized something...I'm in the "Show Business" and so are you. If we don't show our prospects and customers that we care, if we don't show that we have their best interest at heart, if we don't show demonstrations, if we don't show testimonials, if we don't show how our business works, how our products and services work, we won't be in business too long.

We are in show business and today's technology helps us to do this more effectively than ever before in the history of the United States of America.

As I mentioned earlier, you already have the three things you need to be able to show people. You like to help people, you can answer questions or you can interview other experts that can answer questions and you love to share ideas and knowledge. If you have those things, you have all of the tools necessary to do what we're talking about.

Now lets get to this formula. A part of the formula for creating engaging and compelling content is to simply teach and tell powerful and passionate stories of you or how your message is changing lives.

And when people are moved and transformed by your stories and you share proof, inspiration, motivation, and hope...you will be top of mind when they need you or they will refer others who may need you.

When you do this correctly, you start building momentum and developing a following who trust you. And when this "tribe" or "community" of yours is entertained and educated they will buy from you.

The other part of the formula ties right into the second quality of answering questions. Now I can't take the credit for this **GENIUS.** There are others who taught me this simple concept of answering questions and the tremendous impact it has.

So now I want you to write down as many **Frequently Asked Questions,** better known as **FAQs,** as you can.

This does not have to be an all day thing. Just take 5-10 minutes, you'll be surprised how many questions you come up with.

I was talking to a group last night and I said it doesn't necessarily have to be (10) questions. It could be (3) three. It could be (4) four. It could be (5) five. But ideally when I'm consulting with my clients I'd say, "What are the 10 most frequently asked questions that your potential customers, clients or prospects ask you?" What is it they want to know?

Remember, FAQs are questions that people will ask you when they want to know more about a particular area of knowledge or expertise, it is **NOT** about a product or service. So you must resist talking about your products or services.

The goal of the FAQs is to educate without selling. It's about helping them, it's not about you. Ouch! I know that is completely opposite from what the so-called "Sales Guru's" tell you.

You want to give people answers to their questions, but do not hit them with a sales pitch. When you do it this way, you begin to create engagement.

**The FAQs also works with interviewing other experts and celebrities. This is powerful because it also helps to build your brand by association.

Then what you do is answer those questions on video.

"Video?"

Remember that production studio in your pocket. You can record your videos on your Smartphone. You don't have to go and purchase a $500 camera or a $1000 camera.

You can simply turn your phone camera to you and instead of taking "A Selfie", you record a video and answer those questions.

Here's an example, "This is Bro. Bedford, Black America's #1 Internet Marketing Coach, Consultant, & Strategist and the number one question I get asked all the time is 'how do I create engaging and compelling content?'

The first thing you should do is write down the 10 Frequently Asked Questions that your prospects ask you and then video record your answers. You can answer those questions one at a time or you can answer all 10 and then have them edited.

Then you upload those 10 videos to YouTube and other video channels to begin to drive traffic back to your website to capture the leads. If you would like to get 3 more strategies to create engaging and compelling content visit www.brobedford.com".

As you can see the videos don't have to be long, they can be around 3-5 minutes.

Now if you do that and answer those questions, you will see that you'll begin to have your prospects and customers wanting to know more and more and wanting to engage with you. This is how you begin to get traffic back to your site.

The second phase of this are the **SAQs** or **Should Ask Questions -** these are the questions that you know that people who are interested in your expertise or knowledge should ask you...these are the questions that we say, **"PEOPLE DON'T KNOW THAT THEY DON'T KNOW.**

This is your Wisdom and Experience. You may have spent 5, 10, or 20 years studying and working in an area and you develop this knowledge that most people aren't even aware of, especially if they haven't put in the time and work you have.

The difference between FAQs and SAQs is that an FAQ is generally what people are searching for online. Its general information, this is how people are introduced to you and they get to know you.

FAQs are very, very important, but the SAQs are what separate you from anyone else and display your value and make you the expert. **The SAQs demonstrate your passion and expertise and convinces people that you are the solution to their problem.**

I want you to think, really think about this...To gain this **EXPERT, AUTHORITY POSITIONING** in the mind of your targeted audience, all you have to do is answer some questions. How Awesome is that?

When your target audience see you, hear you, and read your material on their smartphones, tablets, computers, televisions, and cars they will trust and believe that you are the answer to their dreams.

Another added benefit, as if you need more, is when the media discovers or is introduced to your engaging and compelling content you start getting calls from radio and television and other experts.

Remember how I told you you can partner with those big brands that control the eyeballs and ears of billions of people?

They control access to billions of people who don't know you or what you do and its important to your business to show these people how your products, services, expertise and experience can help them.

And here's the beautiful part, this can be done with the click of a button for free. Google could be sharing your message to millions of users and it will cost you nothing.

If that excites you, let's dive a little bit deeper into this exciting world of creating your own dynamic platform and connecting to multibillion dollar platforms.

Chapter Eight
Powering Up Your Platform by Leveraging & Distributing Content Thru Billion Dollar Brands!

Ok, in this book I've shared with you how to take Your Knowledge, Experience, Expertise & Passion and turn them into Information Products that you can get paid for.

I've shared with you The Money that can be made from them and I was truly being conservative. I even showed you the Best Way to Sell those products as well.

I've also shared with you The Biggest Business Marketing Challenge facing Business Owners and Entrepreneurs.

I shared with you why you should Leverage and Partner with Billion Dollar Brands and what it would take to do that.

In the last chapter I showed you How To Create Engaging & Compelling Content and the Psychology Behind It.

In this chapter I will reveal to you the Strategies and System that can give you an advantage for leveraging and partnering with the biggest brands in the world.

You'll be able to Drive Traffic to your Site or Business, Capture Leads and Grow Your List and Establish Deeper Relationships with your customers.

And this works 24/7.

You'll learn a fast distribution strategy that will get your story or message out to potentially millions and the best part is you can start ASAP!

Ok, let's dive in....

Webcasting Or LiveCasting

Webcasting, LiveCasting, or LiveStreaming has become the most powerful way to get Traffic, Leads and Sales by leveraging Google Hangouts Online and YouTube Live.

As of this writing, Google reports it is capable of broadcasting to several million viewers simultaneously for free.

This means that you can be Seen and Heard by as many as 1,000,000 viewers on Smartphones, Tablets, Desktops or Laptop Computers and let's not forget Smart TVs live!

This strategy requires minimal equipment and technology. You can charge for webcast or they can be free.

And because you are doing them live, you can have an interactive conversation with your viewers - whether there are 10, 100, 1000 or 100,000 viewers at once.

Broadcast and Television companies are terrified about what is happening with this technology. You can have your own show without the infrastructure and broadcast expenses needed in the past.

Webcast are the future of online selling, content creation, brand building, sharing your message, ideas and growing your list/audience.

Let's take a deeper look at this.

Online Selling has changed over the years. You can still put up a long sales letter and get results, but not as effectively as you could in the past. Yes people are still going to eBay and other online retailers and purchasing products, but normally their mind is made up when they get there, less impulse buys.

Now when people are searching for a product or service the want to be educated about it, they want to see demonstrations and be entertained.

This is like having an Online Interactive Infomercial.

You can do this with Webcasting.

Content Creation. I've already shared with you the importance of creating engaging and compelling content. Good content is not enough anymore.

So you can use the same strategies I showed you to make content, but using a webcast to do it. What do I mean?

You can host a Webcast or LiveCast and answer your FAQS and SAQs. While hosting a Webcast or LiveCast you could turn on the chat and answer questions based on live interaction.

You can literally host a Webcast as a Q&A, and answer the questions from your attendees. Can you imagine what is going on in their minds when they see and hear you answering questions? This leads to the next point...

Brand Building. What better way to build your brand than to answer questions and have people interacting with you live. You're showing them your Expertise. This is how you become the Celebrity Authority in your category.

Growing Your List/Audience. Keep in mind that people should be registering for your Webcast. The more people you get to register, the bigger your list grows. If you are providing great content the more people will share and your audience will expand.

Even if you host a Webcast or LiveCast without building your list on the front end...still deliver great content and then you can drive the people to join your list by offering more information or a gift (remember chapter 3).

And lastly, but definitely not least. **Sharing Your Message and Ideas.** Imagine hosting your own show. Every week you can have a show sharing your message and ideas building an audience that tunes in to see you and your guest.

This is why the Broadcast and Television companies are upset. You will see more and more celebrities hosting their own online shows. It's already happening and you can do the same thing.

You can sell your own products and services from your own show or you can begin to look for advertisers and sponsors. But you have to have a large enough audience to get businesses or companies to sponsor or advertise on your show.

Webcasts or LiveCasts can be recorded and replayed as an encore that can sell your product or service over and over again. You can allow people to view you **ON DEMAND.**

The recording can also be downloaded and then it can be sliced up and cut into smaller videos that can be blasted and distributed to all of the video networks, to all of your social networks, driving traffic back to your site. This is an excellent way to get free traffic to your websites.

Podcasting

The next part or Pillar of the strategy is Podcasting. Podcasting is a great way to create content and drive traffic, generate leads and sales by partnering with Apple.

What is Podcasting? Podcasting or a podcast is simply an mp3 audio or an mp4 video file that is uploaded into iTunes.

You can start your own online radio or television show that can be watched or listened to on any Smartphone, tablet, laptop or desktop computer, Smart TVs and Cars!

Close to 100 million people in America drive back and forth, approximately an hour, to work everyday listening to audio and almost 25% listen to **STREAMING CONTENT or Podcasts.**

Why shouldn't they be listening to your message, your podcast. Listening to you or your guest talking about your products and services for that hour?

When people Subscribe to your Podcast each episode you "Publish" is delivered 100% of the time within minutes. Even email is not delivered 100% of the time.

Once you create a your podcast channel and episodes, Apple will promote you to it's nearly 1.5 billion podcast subscribers, they will distribute your show and you also get a page and website in iTunes...did I mention for **FREE!** C'mon how cool is that.

Here's another jewel...Apple doesn't limit the number of shows you can create so, you could start a radio or TV network for free.

I hear you, I hear you, *"Bro. Bedford, how am I going to create episodes for a Podcast?"* Good Question.

Let me give you a super powerful strategy. Remember the Webcast? You can literally take that same content and create Podcasts.

You can use the same video for a video podcast. It can be edited and spliced to make shorter episodes if you like or you can keep them the same.

You can have the audio taken from the video and now you have an audio podcast. Again the audio can be cut into shorter episodes. So 1 hour long Webcast can be cut into four 15 minute podcast episodes.

It all depends on the niche or category you are in. Some people choose strategies to use audio because maybe there's already a lot of video content based upon the industry that you're in.

Some use the strategy of just using video because there may be a lot of audio content out there. There may be a lot of competition that have audios but no video.

These are ways that you can differentiate yourself in your marketplace.

The bottom line is that you can have your own show, your own online television or radio program that's streaming into the cars of individuals or on smartphones.

Another way to create your show is like thousands of others...You can interview other experts and celebrities. Now before you say, "Who's going to allow me to interview them?" You have to realize that when you have your own show you become media.

Experts and celebrities want to get their messages out to as many people as possible too. So you just have to work to build your audience and the bigger your audience the easier it becomes to get interviews.

Some will give you interviews simply because your mission aligns with their message. I know when I first hatched the idea of interviewing 'Black Millionaire Entrepreneurs' I had my doubts and I had family and friends who didn't mind letting me know that my idea was "crazy".

But I started requesting interviews and I just kept getting yeses. And today from those interviews I have a Podcast, Best-Selling Books, Speaking Engagements, and Relationships with some of Top Entrepreneurs, Business Owners, & Thought Leaders on the planet.

Lastly, you can just speak into a microphone sharing your expertise and ideas. There are tons of shows where the host just speaks on issues and topics that interest their intended audience.

You can record a Podcast on your smartphone or computer. This is the easiest and fastest way to create engaging and compelling content.

Before I close out the section let me just answer a question I get often about Podcast. "How do I make money with Podcast?"

You can monetize podcasts by either getting Sponsors, Advertising Revenue, or you can get income from Driving Your Audience to Direct Sales of your products or services.

Book Publishing

The next pillar of this strategy is **Book Publishing.** What? I thought this was about Digital Product Creation, Internet, Mobile, & Social Media Marketing. "This isn't your Parents Book Publishing."

Amazon has changed the Publishing Game. By partnering with Amazon your book can be read on any Smartphone, tablet, laptop or desktop computer, this can easily translate into more traffic, more leads and more sales.

Remember, when I told you that iTunes will give you a website for your Podcast, Amazon will give you a traffic-producing website too. They will also promote and market you, and get this, Amazon will **PAY YOU** up to **70% commissions on your books they sell for you.**

Did I also mention that Amazon has over 250 Million paying customers in their system. Amazon will sell as many Kindle (digital books/eBooks) or paperback books as you want.

They will promote your books, they will take the orders, they will print your books, they will deliver your books, and as I stated pay you up to 70% royalties. I told you "this is not your parents book publishing".

What would a Best-Selling Book do for your business. Everyone should have a book displaying your expertise. Books are the new business card. Books are still the perfect tool to use to generate qualified leads for any business.

It's much easier to get speaking engagements, get the press involved in what you're doing, to get interviews on Radio and Television if you have a book, if you're a published author.

I hear you, "Bro. Bedford, I can't write a book, that is too hard and will take me forever..." I hear you and I have great news for you.

This is the power of the strategy that I'm sharing with. Remember the Webcast that you performed and recorded. Remember how we said that we can use those videos as video Podcast, remember how we said we can take that audio and have an audio Podcast... well...we can take that same audio and have it transcribed and now you have a book.

You don't have to sit at a desk in a cabin waiting on inspiration to hit you to type out one word at a time. No, take the existing content and repurpose it as a book. Remember those interviews , those interviews can be transcribed. Now you're a published author.

Are you beginning to see the power of this. You have your Content Rich videos on YouTube sharing your expertise. You have you own Podcast on Apple iTunes, your own show further cementing your credibility and authority. Now you have a Best-Selling Book on Amazon being sold all over the world.

You are literally available to Millions of people on their Smartphone, tablet, laptop or desktop computer, Smart TVs and Cars! And you're just getting started, we have to tap into the Power of Social Media.

Using MultiBillion Dollar Social Media Networks to Distribute Your Content

OK, now that you've created Your Webcast, Your Podcast, and Your Book you have to get your message out to the people. Remember, how we talked about answering those questions and then taking that video content and putting in on YouTube. That is not the only place we can distribute our videos and audios.

We can put our messages in front of the audiences of the world's biggest sites like Facebook, Twitter, Linke-dln, Yahoo, Snapchat, Instagram, tumbleUpon, Reddit, Tumbler and many, many more.

See you don't post selfies or bland post...You give people your **FREE** videos and Podcast and excerpts of your books.

And these sites will promote, market, and share you and your message with the world on every Smartphone, tablet, laptop or desktop computer, Smart TVs and Cars!

Now all of this content begins to drive traffic back to your website, your landing page or your business. Once this traffic is driven back to you, you should be capturing the names of individuals so that you can begin to follow up.

That's going to lead me into the last pillar of this strategy.

Mobile Marketing-Building Your List

This is really where the money is made. Once you create your Webcasts, Podcasts, your videos, audios, images, social content, and you distribute through Social Media, your goal should be to capture leads and follow up as many ways as possible.

As I've already mentioned to you that over 75% of the human population is connected using social media. When you add in Smartphones that puts us over 80% of the human population connected and using social media with mobile devices.

More than half of every one who uses social media visits web sites with their smartphones and tablets.

Now what does that mean for your?

Unfortunately, most entrepreneurs and business owners have websites that are not compatible with mobile devices. Most businesses are only capturing leads one way and that is a lead capture form on a website, which will not work if the sites are not mobile compatible.

You must be able to capture leads and follow up with more than just email.

With proper Mobile Marketing, you'll be able to capture leads through multiple channels:

Websites that are mobile responsive
Smartphones
Tablets
Laptop and Desktop Computers
You want to capture with mobile text messages
Short Code
QR Codes

Not only do you want to capture leads through multiple channels, you also want to be able to follow up through multiple channels:

With email
With Mobile Text Messages
With Video Messages

With Audio messages
And Podcast Messages directly into cars or TVs in living rooms!

Summarizing The Power Of This Strategy

There are five pillars of this strategy.

First we talked about Webcasting or LiveCasting where you can create all of the content that you need by hosting live events and answering questions and solving problems. You can also use this strategy to interview experts to offer solutions.

Now there are several platforms that you can use to accomplish this like Go To Meeting, Go To Webinar, UStream, LiveStream and others. But I love Google.

I love Google not only because it's FREE, but it also a Powerful and Simple Platform that you can use immediately. You can open up your account and begin creating your own show…your own network…**LIKE NOW!**

You can take that same content that you created in a Webcast or LiveCast or the YouTube Videos and create an audio file and upload it to your own Podcast Channel on iTunes. Did I mention that iTunes will let you set up a channel for **FREE!**

Ok, now you take that same content and have it transcribed and now you have the content for your book. Now you can upload your book and Self-Publish on Amazon. They have (2) two divisions one is CreateSpace that will allow you to publish your physical book and the other is KDP, which stands for Kindle Direct Publishing, the eBook division.

By the way, did I mention that to open up your accounts on CreateSpace and KDP is **FREE!**

Now you take pieces of that content and distribute that information to your Social Networks, driving people back to your pages, your Videos, your Podcast, your Book page, your landing or lead pages to get people to want more of you.

What business does not want people finding and buying their products and services or calling to their places of business? That's the purpose of Social Media Marketing. Some people really get stumped when it comes to social media and they're doing what they see others doing like posting selfies. This does not translate to Driving Traffic and Building a Brand for your business.

Let's go to the last Pillar of this Amazing Strategy. Creating that compelling content is one thing and now you've began to distribute that content out to iTunes, out to Google and YouTube and through Amazon and now throughout out of all your Social Media Networks like FaceBook, Twitter, and Linkedin.

The whole purpose is to get those individuals coming back to you joining your list so that you can engage with them and develop relationships with them. This is how you get people to support you and your business by buying products and services.

We called this process Mobile Marketing. Why do we call it that? As I already stated, close to 80% of the human populations is connected and using Social Media with Mobile Devices. So you want to be able to build your list with their mobile devices.

And you should be able to do this by texting in, having a QR Code, calling in, or simply entering their name and email on a landing page. The whole purpose is to be able to communicate with them and provide value to them.

This is the most important part of your business, your internet business or your internet marketing strategies, it's really the most important part of your business, period, especially as more and more people go online. You must provide numerous ways for people to get in contact with you and get on your list.

Most people do not have a list. They're not even thinking about building a list, capturing names of people that they can follow up with, that they can continue to deliver compelling content to. And ultimately get those people to support them in their business buying their products or their services.

Good thing that's not you...at least not any more!

Those are the five areas that you should focus on. Now think about this again, creating the content once, distributing it on all of the Multi-Billion dollar platforms, being accessible on all mobile devices.

This is like you being everywhere at the same time - audio, video, written text, blasting that out driving all that traffic and you capturing those names. Then being able to follow up with more education, more training, more content.

Can you see the power of this? Can you see how this changes everything?

This **IS** the future of Marketing.

Chapter Nine
Just Do It…Trust Your Voice!

Ok, we've covered a lot of ground in this book. If I've done my job, you should be clear that you can take your Knowledge, Experience, Expertise, & Passion and package it in a way that can help people and at the same time provide an income and lifestyle that can be fulfilling for you and your family.

You should also know that as an Entrepreneur, Business Owner, Professional, Service Provider, or Author you can spread you Mission, Message, Products, and Services to millions of people and be Seen and Heard on Smartphones, Tablets, Desktops or Laptop Computers, Cars and let's not forget Smart TVs live!

You may be asking yourself, "Can I really do this?"

And the answer is…Absolutely Yes!

Of course like anything else in life that matters, it requires some preparation and implementation and by reading this book you know more about Internet, Mobile, & Social Media Marketing than I did when I started and definitely more than your competitors.

This knowledge that you now possess has allowed me, my students, clients and other entrepreneurs and business owners to generate millions of dollars. I can't wait to see how you use it. Yes, making the money that you want is great, but helping people with your message, products, and services is very rewarding also.

If you watch the news or involved in your community or you just listen to family and friends, you know that people are desperate for help. People are hungry for ideas and strategies to improve their personal and professional lives and they are open to voices who can provide that for them and you can be that voice.

You just have to **Trust Your Voice** and know that people are waiting to hear from you. They want solutions to problems and they want value. And if you give them that they will follow you, support you, and ultimately buy from you.

As I come to the end of this writing. I hope that you've been inspired to Trust Your Voice and Turn Your Knowledge, Experience, Expertise and Passion into information products that can help and serve people and at the same time make more than a comfortable living for you and your family.

I also hope that you have learned how to Leverage and Partner with Multi-Billion Dollar Brands to share your mission, message, products and services to millions of people on their mobile devices, computers, cars, and televisions.

Thank you for allowing me into the conversation going in your head. I'm honored beyond words. If I can be of further assistance, don't hesitate to let me know.

Register This Book and Get Free Updates and Free Videos

To get updates to this book and access to interactive training that will help you implement the strategies in this book to grow your business and an invitation to meet the author, text NOPR to 58885.